THE WATSON GLASER INFERENCE QUESTIONS TINY HANDBOOK

PASSING CRITICAL THINKING TESTS,
VERBAL/LOGICAL REASONING
ASSESSMENTS

LEO MILES

Copyright © 2025 by Leo Miles

All rights reserved.

Version 1.1

No part of this book may be reproduced in any form or by any electronic or mechanical means, including information storage and retrieval systems, without written permission from the author, except for the use of brief quotations in a book review.

For enquiries, contact the author through email: leomilesbooks@mail.com

For all those friends who love to debate over random topics late into the night.

CONTENTS

Preface vii
Structure of the Book ix

PART I
MOST FREQUENTLY SEEN QUESTIONS

Introducing Most Frequently Seen Question Types 3
1. Factual 6
2. Specific-General 9
3. Word Switch 12
4. Future 15
5. Extra Information 17

The Art of Highlighting 21

PART II
WORDING QUESTIONS

Introducing Wording Question Types 25
1. Quantity 27
2. Strength 30
3. Subjective 34

PART III
RELATIONSHIP QUESTIONS

Introducing Relationship Question Types 41
1. Comparison 43
2. Conditional 46
3. Causation 50

PART IV
THEME QUESTIONS

Introducing Theme Question Types 57
1. Conclusion 59

2. Research Study	62
Common Sense Questions	65
Afterword	67
About the Author	69

PREFACE

Hello! Welcome to *The Watson Glaser Inference Questions Tiny Handbook*.

Let's start by talking about what this book is and how you should use it.

This book is written by someone who has sat for countless critical thinking tests, from admissions to law and finance programmes to assessments for commercial law firms and investment banks.

Through the hundreds of tests taken, clear patterns have emerged. Passing the tests became second nature.

There is no secret formula specific to any verbal/logical reasoning assessments or critical thinking tests like the Watson Glaser.

It is a **mindset, a way of thinking**, that leads you to excel in this testing format.

If you master the techniques outlined throughout the *Tiny Handbook*, none of the inference questions on the Watson Glaser will surprise you.

Before you begin, here is a helpful tip as you read through this book.

Pay close attention when the answer is Probably or

Preface

Insufficient Data because it is valuable for you to recognise and understand why they are the correct choice. You will feel much more confident about inference questions because you can detect the *degree* to which the inference applies.

When you are confident about your answer, you are less likely to second-guess yourself and change your answer later on.

There we go, that is all there is to say for now.

So, are you ready?

Let's develop your inference skills!

STRUCTURE OF THE BOOK

For every question type introduced, there will be an example text and a question. After you take the time to think about the text, you can continue reading through our analysis.

Here is the structure of typical Watson Glaser inference questions.

[Text]
[Question]
[Answer Choices: True, Probably True, Insufficient Data, Probably False, False]

When walking you through the answer process, these are the terms the *Tiny Handbook* will use. The question is the statement you are tested on, while the text is the paragraph of writing you read and pick out insights from.

Four Key Elements

The way you should approach questions is as follows. This

Structure of the Book

is the type of thinking you will develop through reading this book.

To understand any inference question, there are four elements you need to know before finalising your answer.

First, you need to identify what type of question it is. Sometimes a question can fit into several categories.

1. What type of question is it?

Basically, you need to know whether the question is straightforward. A question based on facts requires you to simply double-check with the text. Other types of questions require deeper analysis.

An example question: Solaria built the industrial complex in 1993.

You can easily look for years within the text to check.

Second, you need to know why the question was written.

2. Why was the question written?

The purpose of the question will serve as the basis for how you should answer it.

For example: In the Solaria question, you do not have to rely on your common sense. It is a factual question.

The third step is very important.

3. What part of the text is the question targeting?

You must match the wording or the concepts in the question to the text. It could be a word or several sentences.

For example: In the Solaria question, you would look for numerical years in the text. You probably will not need to find support from full sentences.

Finally, you might struggle with picking one answer. That is when the last step comes in.

Structure of the Book

4. What are the trap answers?

For tricky questions, you could be caught between two or three answers because the questions were designed to confuse you. The nuanced wording in the question is the key to picking the correct answer.

Cheat Sheet

If this is your first time picking up the *Tiny Handbook*, this chart will not make sense. But when you have finished reading through it all, you can refer to this chart to remember the different question types.

Question Type	Explanation: Tests your ability to....
Factual	Read the finer details in the text
Specific-General	Notice the slight change in wording, but there is still support
Word Switch	Notice the change in wording, but there is no support
Future	Recognise future statements
Extra Information	Recognise unrelated details
Quantity	Understand the scope of quantity indicators
Strength	Analyse the impact of weak and strong language
Subjective	Recognise opinion statements
Comparison	Identify comparative language
Conditional	Recognise conditional reasoning
Causation	Analyse correlation and causation relationships
Conclusion	Identify the main argument in the text
Research Study	Identify the implications of a study
Common Sense	Think beyond the given text

PART I

MOST FREQUENTLY SEEN QUESTIONS

INTRODUCING MOST FREQUENTLY SEEN QUESTION TYPES

These are the most frequently seen types of inference questions. If you can correctly identify these questions, you will be well on the way to acing the Watson Glaser.

They cover logical fallacies that you have probably thought about already in your daily life.

For example:

Your friend says,
"This soda is so weak! This restaurant chain has the worst soda."

You, the sceptic, think,
"Well, what if this specific store is employing cost-cutting measures and diluting the soda?"

Another example:

Your teacher says,
"Blueberry muffins are so much better than lemon curd muffins. Blueberry muffins are the best muffins ever!"

> You, a blueberry hater, think,
> "What about chocolate chip muffins?"

If you are naturally a sceptic or love to debate, you might annoy your friends and family. But in the world of critical thinking, you are naturally better equipped to succeed. That is because you can intuitively see beyond the words more easily.

But don't worry! If you are not the debater type, this is a skill you can develop with practice.

Here are several actionable steps you can take to improve.

- Read more opinion pieces and essays.
- In your everyday life, listen closely to how people express their ideas. You can see from our above examples that you can learn a lot from banal conversations.
- Study and memorise logical fallacies. You can easily find lists online, and once you get a good grasp of these fallacies, you will recognise them with little thought.

In this part of the book, you will learn five types of questions.

1. Factual: Do you have a basic understanding of the text?
2. Specific-General: Can you recognise slight changes to key words?
3. Word Switch: Can you recognise bigger changes to key words?
4. Future: Can you spot the perspective shift?

5. Extra Information: Do you have a grasp of the subject of the text?

Let's get started!

1
FACTUAL

We will start by talking about the factual questions. These questions are very basic and are intended to be that way.

Most people get these questions right because as long as you fully read the text, you should be able to find the answer. They are testing if you paid attention as you read.

During your test, take what is written in the text as fact. Do not bring your external knowledge to answer the question. What is written in the text is all you know.

Here is an example text and question.

TEXT: Many people believe that video games are a recent form of entertainment. However, the earliest video game came out in 1952. It can be argued that these early games are not analogous to the present understanding of video games. In fact, the first video games were often not created for amusement, but rather for instructional purposes.

QUESTION: Video games were available in 1951.

Remember, your job is to figure out whether the statement is true, probably true, insufficient to conclude, probably false, or false. If you happen to be a video game history expert, throw all your prior knowledge away. Focus only on the given text.

Now let's go through the four elements we mentioned at the start of the book.

1. What type of question is it?
This is a factual question.

2. Why was the question written?
These questions are to test whether you can read closely and pick up the relevant details in the text.

3. What part of the text is the question targeting?
The element of the question that should immediately jump out at you is the year. Skim through the text for mentions of years or any numbers.

4. What are the trap answers?
The traps are the in-between Probably answers. Factual questions are always True or False.

Final Answer
Let's highlight the relevant parts of the text.

TEXT: Many people believe that video games are a recent form of entertainment. However, **the earliest video game came out in 1952**. It can be argued that these early games are not analogous to the present understanding of video games. In fact, the first video games were often not created for amusement, but rather for instructional purposes.

QUESTION: Video games were **available in 1951**.

Read the second sentence of the text. We know that the first video game came out in 1952.

Therefore, the answer is False.

2

SPECIFIC-GENERAL

These questions are pretty easy to spot once you get the hang of them. Basically, it tests a very common flaw where you exaggerate with no basis.

TEXT: Based on genetic testing, Abyssinian cats are likely to have originated in Egypt. Other theories suggest that these cats came from India or Southeast Asia before being developed in the United Kingdom. Abyssinian cats rose in popularity during the 1930s. In current times, Abyssinian cats remain popular at cat shows and have ranked within the top ten of the most popular cat breeds by the Cat Fanciers' Association, the world's largest registry of pedigreed cats.

QUESTION: Abyssinian cats rank within the top ten of popular cat breeds in well-represented registries of pedigreed cats.

1. What type of question is it?
   This is a specific-general question.

2. Why was the question written?
   These questions test your ability to spot the slight shifts in wording.
   For example:

Text Excerpt: The doctors **carefully** picked out the newest medicine on the market for their elderly patients.

Question: The doctors **barely spent any time** picking medicine for their elderly patients.

   The answer is Probably False. The emphasis on the word "carefully" is key because it counters the "barely spent any time". But since there is no concrete information about the time the doctor spent, the answer cannot be False.

3. What part of the text is the question targeting?
   Look out for specific details that are not mentioned in the original text. For example, the introduction of a specific colour, species of animal, or size. Oftentimes, with these questions, they will add or remove a specifier right before the main subject of the sentence.

4. What are the trap answers?
   The traps are the True and False answers. The answers to these questions tend to be Probably True or Probably

False. Occasionally, it can be Insufficient Data, but those tend to fall under a similar category—see *Word Switch*.

Final Answer

By process of elimination, the answer is not True or False because we do not have any information about registries other than the Cat Fanciers' Association.

Now let's highlight relevant parts of the text.

TEXT: Based on genetic testing, Abyssinian cats are likely to have originated in Egypt. Other theories suggest that these cats came from India or Southeast Asia before being developed in the United Kingdom. Abyssinian cats rose in popularity during the 1930s. In current times, Abyssinian cats remain popular at cat shows and have ranked **within the top ten of the most popular cat breeds** by the Cat Fanciers' Association, the **world's largest registry of pedigreed cats**.

QUESTION: Abyssinian cats rank **within the top ten of popular cat breeds** in **well-represented** registries of pedigreed cats.

You are looking for a reason to eliminate the answer Insufficient Data. The key to answering this question is "well-represented", which gives enough support to answer Probably True. The reason is that we already know that the largest registry has Abyssinian cats within the top ten most popular cat breeds.

If the question does not specify "well-represented registries", then it would be way too general and supports the Insufficient Data answer.

3

WORD SWITCH

These questions involve the changing of a word or term. While that seems easy to detect, the switch can be pretty tricky to notice.

TEXT: Air traffic controllers are responsible for managing communications with planes, coordinating takeoffs and landings, and directing air traffic within assigned airspace. Flight plans often change over the course of a flight, and air traffic controllers relay important navigational and meteorological data. The job requires quick decision-making and clear communication skills to ensure aviation safety.

QUESTION: Air traffic controllers are taught to relay bird migration data.

1. What type of question is it?
   This is a word switch question.

. . .

2. Why was the question written?

These questions test your ability to spot the changes in words. If you read quickly, you could miss it.

3. What part of the text is the question targeting?

The easiest way to spot this is to try to match the wording of the question with the text. Some words are interchangeable, but oftentimes it is not possible without changing the meaning significantly.

4. What are the trap answers?

The traps are the True and False answers. Many people fail to notice the switch and believe it directly matches or contradicts the text.

Total word switch questions, unlike specific-general questions, tend to be Insufficient Data.

Final Answer

Let's start with highlighting.

TEXT: Air traffic controllers are responsible for managing communications with planes, coordinating takeoffs and landings, and directing air traffic within assigned airspace. Flight plans often change over the course of a flight, and air traffic controllers relay **important navigational and meteorological data**. The job requires quick decision-making and clear communication skills to ensure aviation safety.

QUESTION: Air traffic controllers are taught to relay **bird migration data**.

Some people might hesitate on this question because they might wonder if "navigational data" includes "bird migration data".

Do not overthink it. What is the normal definition of "navigation"? It is about directions. Imagine a compass. It is not the science of bird behaviour.

The answer is Insufficient Data.

4
FUTURE

The wording of these questions makes them pretty easy to identify. In fact, these questions are among the quicker ones to answer.

TEXT: At the annual meeting, the company revealed plans to release a new line of products that incorporates artificial intelligence agents into existing software. To support these new developments, the company will also invest in data centres and focus on lateral hiring of promising tech talent. Cost-cutting measures will be limited to redundant European offices amidst the shift to working from home.

QUESTION: Over the next five years, the company's new measures will lead to at least a 5 per cent revenue growth.

1. What type of question is it?
   This is a future question.

. . .

2. Why was the question written?

These questions catch people who over-extrapolate and make too many connections. You need to stay within the scope of the question.

For example: Children keep growing taller, but you cannot expect them to keep growing taller forever.

3. What part of the text is the question targeting?

Look at the sentence or sentences in the text that the question is referencing and read carefully. Does it say anything about the future? Or is it merely referencing what is happening in the present?

4. What are the trap answers?

The traps are the Probably True and Probably False answers. Don't overstep and assume that what's going on now will happen in the future!

The answer is usually Insufficient Data.

Final Answer

You can figure out the answer by looking at the question only.

QUESTION: **Over the next five years**, the company's new measures will lead to at least a 5 per cent revenue growth.

You cannot deduce the future! So many factors cannot be accounted for. What if the new products are not popular? What if there is a recession or a pandemic?

The answer is Insufficient Data.

5
EXTRA INFORMATION

You should identify these questions very quickly because they are often outlandish and completely unrelated to the text.

TEXT: Hatshepsut was a female pharaoh in ancient Egypt in the 15th century BC. She ruled for over 2 decades, successfully gaining power through the support of influential officials. Her prominent policies include establishing trade networks to obtain valuable goods such as ivory and incense and commissioning construction projects such as the temple of Pakhet at Beni Hasan. Her success as a ruler is well known today, and artefacts produced under her reign exist in museums around the world.

QUESTION: Hatshepsut commissioned the early model of the modern toilet.

1. What type of question is it?
   This is an extra information question.

. . .

2. Why was the question written?
This question tests your ability to skim the text.

3. What part of the text is the question targeting?
It should be very clear that the question is bringing in new information. If you are reading the question and thinking, "Where the heck did this come from?", then you know it is an extra information question.

4. What are the trap answers?
Some people might try to imply something from the original text and answer Probably True or Probably False. But the answer is Insufficient Data.

Final Answer
Let's look at the question.

QUESTION: Hatshepsut commissioned the **early model of the modern toilet**.

You need to look for anything in the text about a toilet or even modern sanitary hardware.

TEXT: Hatshepsut was a female pharaoh in ancient Egypt in the 15th century BC. She ruled for over 2 decades, successfully gaining power through the support of influential officials. Her prominent policies include establishing trade networks to obtain valuable goods such as ivory and incense and **commissioning construction projects**

such as the temple of Pakhet at Beni Hasan. Her success as a ruler is well known today, and artefacts produced under her reign exist in museums around the world.

While Hatshepsut did commission things, all we know is that she commissioned construction projects like temples.
The answer is Insufficient Data.

THE ART OF HIGHLIGHTING

In the first part of the book, you would have noticed the highlighting of specific words in the texts and questions when explaining the final answer. Hopefully, the visual cues helped you spot the key parts that lead to the correct answer.

When you complete your test, you will probably work on a computer or digital device where highlighting is not possible. But during the learning process, it is helpful for you to practice emphasising the important parts of the text.

Issue spotting is a key skill for being an effective lawyer. Once you get the hang of how to think about these questions, you will be able to quickly pick up what you are being tested on.

So during your practice sessions, print out your practice tests and take the time to analyse the text given the context of each question before considering the answers.

This is a very important step in boosting your understanding.

Moving forward, the value of highlighting will become

The Art of Highlighting

even clearer. As the difficulty of the questions goes up, the nuances of the answers will require careful reading and emphasis.

PART II

WORDING QUESTIONS

INTRODUCING WORDING QUESTION TYPES

The *Tiny Handbook* has repeatedly reiterated the importance of identifying specific words. So, what is the point of having a separate part on wording?

A separate part is needed because there are certain words that you should flag immediately the moment you read the question.

Read through these statements.

- <u>Some</u> people can juggle five glass bottles.
- <u>Most</u> fans are navy blue.
- Sheila <u>can</u> go to the store today before her doctor's appointment.
- Squirrels <u>must</u> carry food in their cheeks while they run.
- Lawyers <u>should</u> always act ethically.
- Friends <u>should</u> <u>always</u> treat each other with respect.

Once you build up the habit of noticing these words,

you can swiftly spot any issues and move on to the next question.

The scope of these words is very commonly tested in critical thinking assessments. Properly identifying them is imperative to your success and will help build careful reading habits.

There are three categories you need to know.

1. Quantity: What is the difference between "some" and "most"?
2. Strength: What is the distinction between "can" and "must"?
3. Subjective: When is "should" used?

A quick tip: Do not get too caught up in categorising where words fit between the three categories. There is a lot of overlap. The important part is that you can flag the word and compare it with the tested part in the text.

1
QUANTITY

Peek down at the lists of words! The strategy for these questions mainly involves memorisation. You should be fine if you know which quantity words fit in the same category.

TEXT: Groupthink occurs when poor decisions are made as a group because group members hold back dissenting opinions to conform. As a result, decisions are tainted by bias, and alternative considerations are not considered properly. However, not all cases of groupthink result in poor decisions. In certain contexts, groupthink may spur quicker decision making and spur confidence.

QUESTION: Despite the potential benefits, groupthink can cause many poor decisions.

1. What type of question is it?
   This is a quantity question.

. . .

2. Why was the question written?

These questions check your understanding of the scope of quantity words.

Here is the table you have to memorise. The words in the same list are interchangeable.

Some refers to anything over 0% (including 100%).

>some
>many
>several
>a few
>occasionally
>sometimes
>regularly
>often
>not all

Most refers to anything over 50%.

>most
>more than half
>majority
>nearly all
>almost all
>typically
>usually
>generally
>tend to
>few

For example: Something that is <u>regularly</u> used may not be <u>generally</u> used.

3. What part of the text is the question targeting?

The quantity indicators are the target.

4. What are the trap answers?

A common mistake is thinking "some" and "many" are different. Also, be careful about the word "often".

Final Answer

This question hinges on proper highlighting. When you finish the book, you will recognise the importance of the other highlights (see the *Strength* and *Causation* sections).

TEXT: Groupthink occurs when poor decisions are made as a group because group members hold back dissenting opinions to conform. As a result, decisions are tainted by bias, and alternative considerations are not considered properly. However, **not all** cases of groupthink **result** in poor decisions. In certain contexts, groupthink may spur quicker decision making and spur confidence.

QUESTION: Despite the potential benefits, groupthink **can cause many** poor decisions.

The text's second-to-last sentence is the focus of this question. Does "not all" equate to "many"?
Check the list.
It absolutely does!
So the answer is True.
Also, the "can" makes it very easy to answer because it is weak language. That brings us to the next section.

2

STRENGTH

Strength questions are not as common as the other two sections in this part of the book. Regardless, you definitely should look out for this question type.

TEXT: The advertising campaign for the company's jeans is likely to be deemed successful. The new marketing manager has close ties to most fashion magazines and is focussing on the company's sponsored partners at Paris Fashion Week. Social media campaigns have high engagement rates without overly high spending.

QUESTION: The company's advertising campaign has increased the sales of some jeans.

1. What type of question is it?
   This is a strength question.

2. Why was the question written?

The Watson Glaser Inference Questions Tiny Handbook

These questions test careful reading and your ability to spot strength words. You must understand the distinction between weak and strong language.

You do not exactly need to memorise these words. If you can spot the distinction in wording strength, it should be intuitive when you read the statement. That takes practice.

Here are several words that fit in either category:

Weak indicators:
can
could
might
some

Strong indicators:
must
all
never
always

If there is strong language in the text, the answer can be weak. But if there is weak language in the text, the answer cannot be strong.

For example:

Text Excerpt #1: At the company, the candies **must** be placed in packaging matching the colour of the design.
Text Excerpt #2: At the company, **some** candies are placed in packaging matching the colour of the design.

Question #1: **Some** candies have packages matching the colour of the design.

Question #2: The candies have packaging that matches the colour of the design.

Question #1 has weak language and can be inferred from either of the text excerpts.

On the other hand, Question #2 has much stronger language. It implies that all the candies have packaging that matches the colour of the design. This can only be inferred from Text Excerpt #1.

3. What part of the text is the question targeting?
Look for strong and weak words. Once you get the hang of it, you will sense that the question is too strong and can answer immediately.

4. What are the trap answers?
Some people miss the weak words like "some" or fail to notice the implied "all" as seen in the example above with Question #2.

Take a moment and think about what the question is saying. How certain is the statement?

If the question has strong language, it needs a lot of support for it to be True or False.

If the question is weak, there is likely enough support for the answer to not be Insufficient Data.

Final Answer
Let's start with highlighting.

TEXT: The **advertising campaign** for the company's jeans is **likely** to be deemed successful. The new marketing manager has close ties to most fashion magazines and is focussing on the company's sponsored partners at Paris Fashion Week. Social media campaigns have high engagement rates without overly high spending.

QUESTION: The company's advertising campaign has increased the **sales** of **some** jeans.

The question has quite weak language, which suggests that we will not have an Insufficient Data answer. Note that the text does not mention anything about jeans sales.

However, the first sentence supports the effectiveness of the advertising campaign. And an effective campaign would likely lead to an increase in sales. This is not definitive, so the answer is Probably True.

Fun Fact:
If you have done other types of verbal reasoning tests (notably SHL), which have True/Cannot Say/False answers, the answer to this question would be Cannot Say.

With the Watson Glaser, you have a tougher task to differentiate between the Probably and Insufficient Data answers.

3
SUBJECTIVE

Compared to the other two sections in the *Wording* part, this one is simpler.

TEXT: Nations around the world are suffering from low voter turnout. A notable counter to this trend is Malta, often with over 80 per cent voter turnout without mandatory voting. As governments must enact policies that reflect the public interest, there should be efforts to increase voter participation. Measures such as online voting can eliminate barriers for overseas citizens, remote residents, and people with disabilities. However, security concerns have hindered the popularity of online voting.

QUESTION: It is too difficult to encourage citizens to vote, so governments should focus on properly expressing their platforms to the citizens who do.

1. What type of question is it?
   This is a subjective question.

The Watson Glaser Inference Questions Tiny Handbook

. . .

2. Why was the question written?

An important word to recognise for subjective questions is "should". Other words that could fall under this category are "need" and "must", but these also fall under strength questions.

Remember that if the given text does not present an argument or point of view, there is no valid subjective inference.

3. What part of the text is the question targeting?

Look for an opinion in the question. "Should" or "arguably" are good signs.

4. What are the trap answers?

Be careful and do not bring in your viewpoints when answering critical thinking questions. Assess the question based on its own merits.

The answer is usually Insufficient Data unless the main theme of the text supports the inference. See the *Theme Questions* part to understand this distinction.

Final Answer

Let's take a look at the question.

QUESTION: It is **too difficult** to encourage citizens to vote, so governments **should** focus on properly expressing their platforms to the citizens who do.

Even if you are not actively looking for subjective

words, it is clear that this is an opinion statement. The next step is to figure out whether this opinion can be inferred from the text.

TEXT: Nations around the world are suffering from low voter turnout. A notable counter to this trend is Malta, often with over 80 per cent voter turnout without mandatory voting. As governments **must** enact policies that reflect the public interest, there **should** be efforts to increase voter participation. Measures such as online voting can eliminate barriers for overseas citizens, remote residents, and people with disabilities. However, security concerns have hindered the popularity of online voting.

With the highlighted words, we can see there is some subjective wording in the text. But is this sentence an important part of the text? Is it a key part of what the text is arguing for?
No, it provides context for the argument.
Here is the structure of the text:

[Context: low voter turnout, so increase voter participation]
[Premise 1: online voting]
[Premise 2: but security concerns]

The question is inferring a very specific solution to this issue, focussing on the voting citizens, which is not supported by the text.
Here are two inferences that can be supported:

- Other methods, other than online voting, could be explored to increase voting participation.

- Online voting may not be the best way to increase voter turnout.

You might notice how weak and general the language is in these examples.

The answer is Insufficient Data.

PART III

RELATIONSHIP QUESTIONS

INTRODUCING RELATIONSHIP QUESTION TYPES

The last two parts of the *Tiny Handbook* move away from spotting key words. You will need to analyse full sentences or even the whole chunk of text.

In this part, you will learn to recognise relationships in sentences.

The three relationships you must know are:

1. Comparison: Can you recognise when two ideas are being compared in a statement?
2. Conditional: Do you have a basic understanding of conditional statements?
3. Causation: Can you spot causation relationships?

Another way to represent the three relationships is through these examples:

1. Comparison: Horses have more legs than humans.
2. Conditional: If movies were real, history would be hard to interpret.

3. Causation: The sprinkler made the grass wet.

Honestly, relationship questions sound much tougher than they actually are. The best way to introduce these ideas is by working through the questions.

So let's go!

1
COMPARISON

Comparison questions consider differences and similarities between two things.

TEXT: A new study has established that the new medicine can revolutionise cancer research by targeting how the cancer cells adapt to withstand treatment. This method does not kill the cancer cells directly. Doctors involved in the study are confident that there will be positive results during clinical trials.

QUESTION: The new medicine is more effective than medicines that kill cancer cells directly.

1. What type of question is it?
   This is a comparison question.

2. Why was the question written?

These questions test your ability to distinguish comparisons rather than absolutes. Do not mix up the two.

For example:

Text Excerpt: The granite is larger than the cobalt.

Question: The granite is the largest.

The text excerpt considers the granite's size relative to the cobalt. On the other hand, the question makes an absolute claim.

Now, what if the text and question are switched?

Text Excerpt: The granite is the largest.

Question: The granite is larger than the cobalt.

This works. It is known that the granite is the largest, so it is clear that it is larger than the cobalt.

3. What part of the text is the question targeting?
You should look out for "than" to quickly identify comparisons. Then, you can look for a similarly worded sentence in the given text.

4. What are the trap answers?
As mentioned earlier, do not make the common mistake of inferring absolutes from relative comparisons. The answer is often Insufficient Data.

However, you can have a True or False answer when inferring from absolutes.

. . .

Final Answer

Rather than focussing just on the question, we can work through this question by highlighting both the text and the question.

TEXT: A new study has established that the new medicine can **revolutionise** cancer research by targeting how the cancer cells adapt to withstand treatment. This method does not kill the **cancer cells** directly. Doctors involved in the study are confident that there will be positive results during clinical trials.

QUESTION: The new medicine is **more effective than** medicines that kill **cancer cells** directly.

This question is comparative.

We now have to look at the text for anything about relative effectiveness. What is mentioned is revolutionising cancer research and that the new method does not kill cancer cells directly.

It appears that this is a new method, which is why it is revolutionary, not necessarily because it is an improvement over the previous method.

The answer is Insufficient Data.

2

CONDITIONAL

If you have studied logical reasoning before, then you will have no problems with this section at all.

TEXT: Three people were brought in for questioning as part of a police investigation. Sally was the only person who lied during the investigation. She spoke more than the other two people and made up facts about the crime scene. However, news reports erroneously reported that all three of them had lied.

QUESTION: If Sally told the truth, news reports would still report that she lied.

1. What type of question is it?
   This is a conditional question.

2. Why was the question written?

The Watson Glaser Inference Questions Tiny Handbook

These questions test your understanding of conditional reasoning.

You should be aware of two structures.

1. If-then statements: If Peter makes me tea, then tell him to add cream and sugar.
2. Only statements: Only candy can make the baby stop crying. (An alternative way to write this is: The baby will stop crying only when given candy.)

You can quickly diagram if-then statements.

1. Peter makes me tea -> tell Peter to add cream and sugar

As long as Peter makes my tea, he will be told about the cream and sugar. The left part of the chain, if satisfied, is sufficient to trigger the necessary right part of the chain.

Now convert the example only statement to the if-then structure.

2. If the baby stops crying, it was given candy.

Baby stops crying -> given candy

We know that candy is necessary to make the baby stop crying. Therefore, it is on the right side.

Now, here is the one rule you need to remember about conditional statements. **You cannot switch the sufficient and necessary.**

For instance, you cannot infer that the baby would stop crying if you give it candy.

That diagram looks like this:

given candy -> baby stops crying

The original statement is saying that if the baby stops crying, it definitely was given candy. But the baby may continue crying even after being given candy.

3. What part of the text is the question targeting?
Look for if-then statements or only statements.

4. What are the trap answers?
Do not switch the sufficient and necessary! This is an extremely common mistake in logical reasoning. When people fail to notice the switch, they might answer True or False when the answer is Insufficient Data.

Final Answer
This question will help you better understand conditional reasoning.

QUESTION: **If** Sally told the truth, news reports would still report that she lied.

This is an if-then statement. The "then" is often not explicit, which is fine.
To support this inference, the sufficient must be triggered. In the text, it should mention Sally telling the truth.

TEXT: Three people were brought in for questioning as part of a police investigation. **Sally was the only person who lied during the investigation. She spoke more than the other two people and made**

The Watson Glaser Inference Questions Tiny Handbook

up facts about the crime scene. However, news reports erroneously reported that all three of them had lied.

There is nothing in the text about Sally being truthful. All we know is what actually happened during the investigation. So, the statement in the question has no support.

The answer is Insufficient Data.

Conditional questions are similar to future questions. You simply cannot know what has not or will not happen.

3

CAUSATION

When the sentence in the text establishes a relationship, it is often a causation relationship. While causation is not always tested, you should be aware of the concept.

TEXT: After the release of its latest line of toys, Carmen Company is facing allegations of intellectual property infringement. There are also claims that the toy contains small parts that constitute a choking hazard. Carmen Company's stock price was already down 20 per cent before it fell another 30 per cent when the news broke. Analysts are revising earnings estimates, and the company will hold a press conference next Thursday.

QUESTION: The allegations of intellectual property infringement and the potential choking hazard are the main reasons Carmen Company's stock price is struggling.

1. What type of question is it?

This is a causation question.

2. Why was the question written?

These questions want you to understand causation. You must recognise when any of the sentences are referencing causation.

Another important concept is that correlation does not imply causation.

To illustrate this distinction:

Correlation: When the car honks, Kevin is **likely** to run out of the house.

Causation: **Because** the car honks, he runs out of the house.

For the first statement, you can think of many other reasons he ran out of the house. Maybe his friend always texts him first, and that is what Kevin is responding to. Perhaps his friend is always on time, and Kevin runs out at 9 am sharp.

In the second statement, it is explicitly stated that Kevin runs out because of the car honk.

Here are words that establish correlation and causation relationships:

Correlation indicators:
associated with
coincides
tends
often
likely
associated with

Causation indicators:
due to
made
because
a result of
contributes to
leads to
stimulates
causes
induces
produces
is a factor
has the effect
a consequence of

3. What part of the text is the question targeting?

You should be able to identify causation in the statement. Usually, it is intuitive, but the list of words might be helpful to you.

Do not worry too much about correlation. Correlation statements can always be conditional statements.

4. What are the trap answers?

Failing to notice causation relationships in the text means you might miss certain True or False answers. If you mistake correlation for causation, then you might erroneously answer True or False when it should be Insufficient Data.

The text might also try to trick you into thinking there is a causal relationship when there are other realistic causes.

The Watson Glaser Inference Questions Tiny Handbook

. . .

Final Answer

This is a less conventional causation question because the prior examples cover the basic idea.

TEXT: After the release of its latest line of toys, Carmen Company is facing allegations of intellectual property infringement. There are also claims that the toy contains small parts that constitute a choking hazard. Carmen Company's stock price was **already down 20 per cent before it fell another 30 per cent** when the news broke. Analysts are revising earnings estimates, and the company will hold a press conference next Thursday.

QUESTION: The allegations of intellectual property infringement and the potential choking hazard are **the main reasons** Carmen Company's stock price is struggling.

For this question, think about what exactly caused Carmen Company's stock price to fall. We know that the stock price had already fallen 20 per cent before the news was announced. There was likely another reason.

Perhaps the culmination of all the factors led to the stock price falling another 30 per cent. Or maybe the news of the allegations caused the 30 per cent drop.

We have no idea what the main reason was, but it seems like the stock price was already doing poorly.

The answer is Probably False.

PART IV
THEME QUESTIONS

INTRODUCING THEME QUESTION TYPES

This part differs from the rest of the *Tiny Handbook*. Rather than looking at the wording, you must draw out the main message or theme of the text. The two types of theme questions are:

1. Conclusion: What is the author trying to convey?
2. Research Study: What are the results of the study?

The first step is to figure out whether the text qualifies for theme questions. If the text is merely relaying information like a paragraph in an encyclopaedia, it is not designed to test you on the theme.

For instance, these three statements have different tones.

Statement 1: Dogs are descended from an extinct population of grey wolves.

Statement 2: The students should not be reading in the dark to avoid straining their eyes.

Statement 3: Studies show that the meal replacement drink can lead to high blood pressure.

Statement 1 is purely informative, while Statement 2 is opinionated and has taken a stance. Statement 3 is relaying results from a study.

This part of the book deals with the latter two statements, which are more than merely informative.

Once you know the text qualifies for theme questions, the next step is to predict the conclusion or study results. While it may be tempting to read the question immediately, focus on the text and come up with your prediction. It is easy to be influenced by the question.

Let's draft predictions for Statements 2 and 3.

Statement 2: Students should avoid straining their eyes.

Statement 3: People who have overly high blood pressure should avoid the meal replacement drink.

There is no right answer, of course, because it was not already written in the text! As long as your answer makes sense, you can move on to the question.

Now let's jump straight to the question types.

1
CONCLUSION

Conclusion questions feel like classic inference questions, where you are tasked with coming up with deeper insights from a piece of writing.

TEXT: Over the past two weeks, the lake has developed a strange orange growth. City officials immediately restricted all people from entering the water or consuming anything from the lake. The lake has been subjected to years of illegal dumping of toxic waste, which has been ignored due to the lobbying of powerful factory owners.

QUESTION: The lake is polluted and requires urgent action.

1. What type of question is it?
    This is a conclusion question.

2. Why was the question written?

These questions test your ability to draw out the conclusion or the main point of the text.

3. What part of the text is the question targeting?

You will need to determine which parts are crucial in determining the main point. Read carefully and try to come up with one more sentence to wrap up the text. That will be the conclusion.

For example:

Text: Last week, the family cleaned the house and the yard before going on a trip. Everything looked sparkling clean. When they got back, they saw dirt all over the patio deck.

To come up with a conclusion, picture this text as incomplete. It is missing an ending sentence.

What are the possible conclusions?

- The neighbour's dog walked on the patio deck.
- There was a windy storm over the weekend.
- Delivery drivers left several packages on the patio deck while the family was gone.

It is also possible that the text already has a conclusion. In that case, you can compare the explicit conclusion with the question.

4. What are the trap answers?

You might come to an incorrect conclusion if you did not read carefully enough.

. . .

Final Answer

Let's start with the text.

TEXT: Over the past two weeks, the lake has developed a strange orange growth. City officials **immediately** restricted all people from entering the water or consuming anything from the lake. The lake has been subjected to years of illegal dumping of toxic waste, which has been ignored due to the lobbying of powerful factory owners.

You should notice that the text feels unfinished. It is missing a conclusion. We can brainstorm several right away.

- The orange growth in the lake likely arose from the illegal dumping.
- The orange growth might be unsafe.

Now let's look at the question.

QUESTION: The lake is polluted and **requires** urgent action.

The first part about pollution is very general, which makes it easy to support. The second part is tougher, but it is supported by the fact that the city officials acted immediately.

The answer is True.

2
RESEARCH STUDY

These questions are very recognisable because they either explicitly mention a study or are scientifically focussed.

TEXT: Businesses that heavily rely on digital markets are always looking for more effective monetisation strategies. In a recent study, it was discovered that people were more inclined to purchase add-ons to online microtransactions when the advertisements were less frequent and more personalised.

QUESTION: Businesses can increase digital monetisation revenue by personalising advertisements and displaying them less frequently.

1. What type of question is it?
    This is a research study question.

. . .

2. Why was the question written?

These questions will establish whether you can conclude the results of the study or piece of research. You can quickly get a sense of what the results are by thinking about what the evidence supports.

3. What part of the text is the question targeting?

As mentioned above, look at the evidence mentioned.

4. What are the trap answers?

Do not answer True or False for overly broad inferences. Those would be Probably True or Probably False. More specific answers would be True or False.

For example, the study might focus on a specific city like York. An inference that references York would be more likely to be True or False compared to an inference about England.

Final Answer

To answer this question, let's consider what the study results are.

TEXT: Businesses that heavily rely on digital markets are always looking for more effective monetisation strategies. In a recent study, it was discovered that **people were more inclined to purchase add-ons to online microtransactions when the advertisements were less frequent and more personalised**.

It is establishing a relationship between the sale of add-ons and the presentation of online advertisements.

QUESTION: Businesses **are likely to** increase digital monetisation revenue by **personalising advertisements and displaying them less frequently**.

Notice how the question is not focussed on add-ons or micro transactions? It is generalising from the study results.

Suddenly, this became a specific-general question.

It is pretty clear the answer is not definite, such as True or False. Let's now consider whether the answer is Insufficient Data.

Is there enough support?

The important point to notice is that the question uses weak language. You should immediately spot the weak "are likely to" rather than a stronger word like "will".

We do not know if all businesses with digital strategies have microtransactions. However, if they do, they will be positively affected by following the results of the study.

Since there is support, but not absolute certainty, the answer is Probably True.

COMMON SENSE QUESTIONS

This brief section is for the answers that do not follow the reasoning demonstrated by the other parts of this book. Those answers are supported by common sense.

Common sense reasoning allows the test makers to choose between the Insufficient Data and the Probably answer choices. Many people make mistakes when choosing between these answers. The nuances between them can be tough to decipher.

When you read the question, ask yourself, "Is there any support for this?"

As you would have noticed throughout this book, you cannot support:

- Statements that have not happened.
- Statements that are completely unrelated.

Without support, the answer can only be Insufficient Data.

But sometimes there is some support, such as in:

- Statements that overgeneralise.
- Statements that are common sense.

In these cases, the answer would be Probably True or Probably False.

Common sense statements are based on one word or term within the text. These words have built-in inferences based on what the average person should already know.

Here are several examples you should recognise:

- **Research** implies peer review.
- A **ban** indicates some level of enforcement.
- Something that is done **voluntarily**, explicitly **chosen**, or **decided** implies the person's interest in that thing.
- **Professionals** like doctors and lawyers are expected to have a level of expertise.
- **Children** and **teenagers** are not expected to be interested in history or world events, but are more adept with technology than **the elderly**.

With practice, you will be able to flag these words the moment you read the question.

AFTERWORD

Thank you again for picking up *The Watson Glaser Inference Questions Tiny Handbook*!

Now that you have finished the book, hopefully you better understand inference questions on the Watson Glaser Test.

A big part of the preparatory process is learning to read more carefully and notice details within the text. As mentioned at the beginning of the book, you can build these skills as you read the news (*The Financial Times* or *The Economist* are good options!) or converse with your friends.

Once you make it a habit to notice specific words or missing conclusions, you will find your assessments much simpler.

Good luck on your legal journey!

ABOUT THE AUTHOR

When not thinking about the law, Leo Miles is a lover of philosophy, economics, and hot tea. Before law, he had experience in the banking sector. He enjoys quality time with his dog and reading widely.

Contact Miles through email: leomilesbooks@mail.com

www.ingramcontent.com/pod-product-compliance
Lightning Source LLC
Chambersburg PA
CBHW071253070526
44583CB00017B/2446